RUGBY SHORTS

MARK LYNCH

HarperCollins*Publishers*

HarperCollins*Publishers*

First published in 2011
by HarperCollins*Publishers* (New Zealand) Limited
PO Box 1, Shortland Street, Auckland 1140

HarperCollins*Publishers*

31 View Road, Glenfield, Auckland 0627, New Zealand
Level 13, 201 Elizabeth Street, Sydney, NSW 2000, Australia
A 53, Sector 57, Noida, UP, India
77–85 Fulham Palace Road, London W6 8JB, United Kingdom
2 Bloor Street East, 20th floor, Toronto, Ontario M4W 1A8, Canada
10 East 53rd Street, New York, NY 10022, USA

National Library of New Zealand Cataloguing-in-Publication Data

Lynch, Mark.
Rugby shorts / Mark Lynch.
ISBN 978-1-86950-950-7
1. Rugby Union football—Caricatures and cartoons. 2. Rugby
Union football—Humor. Title.
741.56994—dc 22

ISBN: 978 1 86950 950 7

Cover and internal design by Mark Lynch

Printed by Printlink, New Zealand

This publication is printed on paper pulp sourced from sustainably grown and managed
forests, using Elemental Chlorine Free (ECF) bleaching, and printed with 100 per cent
vegetable-based inks.

And in the beginning...

'In 1823, William Webb Ellis first picked the ball in his arms and ran with it. And for the next 156 years forwards have been trying to work out why.'

— *Sir Tasker Watkins, 1979*

'For an 18-month suspension,
I feel I probably should have
torn it off. Then at least I could
say, look, I've returned to South
Africa with the guy's ear.'

— *Johan le Roux, on biting*
Sean Fitzpatrick's ear

'If I lie in hospital and I hear they
are putting someone's head back
on that was ripped off by Schalk,
then I'd say:"That's Schalk, he
plays aggressive but he's not
malicious."'

— *Peter de Villiers,*
South African coach

'Rugby is a game for the mentally deficient … that is why it was invented by the British. Who else but an Englishman could invent an oval ball?'

— *Peter Cook*

'They think we're just a bunch of ignorant Paddies from the bog. Let's not disappoint them.'

— *Stewart McKinney, Irish player, before a match against England*

'In my time, I've had my knee out, broken my collarbone, had my nose smashed, a rib broken, lost a few teeth, and ricked my back; but as soon as I get a bit of bad luck I'm going to quit the game.'

— *J.W. Robinson*

'Sure there have been injuries and deaths in rugby – but none of them serious.'

— *'Doc' Mayhew*

'The tactical difference between Association Football and Rugby with its varieties seems to be that in the former the ball is the missile, in the latter men are the missiles.'

— *Alfred E. Crawley,* The Book of the Ball, *1913*

'O'Callaghan, you're boring!'
 — *Referee's infringement call*

'You're not too entertaining yourself, ref.'

— *Phil O'Callaghan, former Irish prop*

'I never comment on referees and I'm not going to break the habit of a lifetime for that prat.'

— *Ewan McKenzie*

'I think you enjoy the game more if you don't know the rules. Anyway, you're on the same wavelength as the referee.'

— *Jonathan Davies*

'Players and spectators at all levels can enjoy sport better if they totally accept two simple rules. Rule 1: The referee is always right. Rule 2: In the event of the referee being obviously wrong, Rule 1 applies.'

— Peter Corrigan

'The problem with referees is that they just don't care which side wins.'

— Tom Canterbury

16

'I don't like this new law, because your first instinct when you see a man on the ground is to go down on him.'

— Murray Mexted

'Leonard! Leonard, you fat bastard! You don't need a physio, you need a f*****g midwife!'

— Will Carling recalls a sledge from the Irish crowd as prop Jason Leonard was receiving treatment

'Rugby football is a game for gentlemen of all classes, but never for a bad sportsman in any class.'

— *Motto of the Barbarians Rugby Football Club*

'Rugby is a game for barbarians played by gentlemen. Football is a game for gentlemen played by barbarians.'

— *Oscar Wilde*

'Rugby is a wonderful show:
dance, opera and suddenly,
the blood of a killing.'

— Richard Burton

'I prefer rugby to soccer. I enjoy
the violence in rugby, except
when they start biting each
other's ears off.'

— Elizabeth Taylor

Bill McLaren, Scotsman, 1923–2010,
BBC commentator, 'The Voice of Rugby'

'A frank exchange of opinions between the gentlemen of the front row.'

— *During an on-field punch-up*

'He's like Bambi on speed.'

— *On Simon Geoghegan*

'They say down at Stradey that if you ever catch him, you get to make a wish.'

— *On Phil Bennett*

'I'm no hod carrier but I would be laying bricks if he was running at me.'

— *On Jonah Lomu*

'Born when meat was cheap.'

— *On big Vleis Visagie*

'Oh mercy me! What a tackle! That could've put him in Ward 4!'

— *Bill McLaren*

'I hope not, Bill, that's a maternity ward.'

— *Fellow commentator*

'I've had four calls from my aunty in the middle of the night calling me a poofter.'

— *Frank Bunce appeals to coach John Hart to drop his 'don't retaliate' stance after copping a barrage of punches without responding*

'They [the All Blacks] kicked the hell out of me in the test. But they were nice blokes.'

— *Harold Tolhurst, 1931 Wallaby*

'The Australians were a great crowd. They'd kick your head off on the ground but they were the best chaps in the world off it.'

— *Alf Waterman, 1929 All Black*

'I met Jonah Lomu. I never knew how huge he was. I felt like a peasant in a Godzilla movie. "Quickly! Tell the other villagers! We go now."'

— *Robin Williams*

'Fijian fullback Waisele Serevi thinks "tackle" is something you take fishing with you.'

— *Jonathan Davies*

'Remember that rugby is a team game; all fourteen of you make sure that you pass the ball to Jonah.'

— *Anonymous fax sent to the New Zealand team at the 1995 World Cup in South Africa*

'Me? As England's answer to Jonah Lomu? Joanna Lumley, more likely.'

— *Damian Hopley, 1995*

'Rugby is a game for big buggers. If you're not a big bugger, you get hurt. I wasn't a big bugger but I was a fast bugger and therefore I avoided the big buggers.'

— *Spike Milligan*

'Ballroom dancing is a contact sport. Rugby is a collision sport.'

— *Heyneke Meyer*

'I can tell you it's a magnificent sensation when the gap opens up like that and you just burst right through.'

— *Murray Mexted*

'Of course it worries me if the All Blacks are invincible. I mean, it stands to reason, if we can't see them, how can we beat them?'

— *Unknown English rugby player*

'Scorpio: there will soon come
a time when your happiness
depends on where and whether
an enormous man catches a ball.'

— *Horoscope from the* Onion

'The only thing you're ever likely
to catch on the end of an English
backline is chilblains.'

— *David Campese*

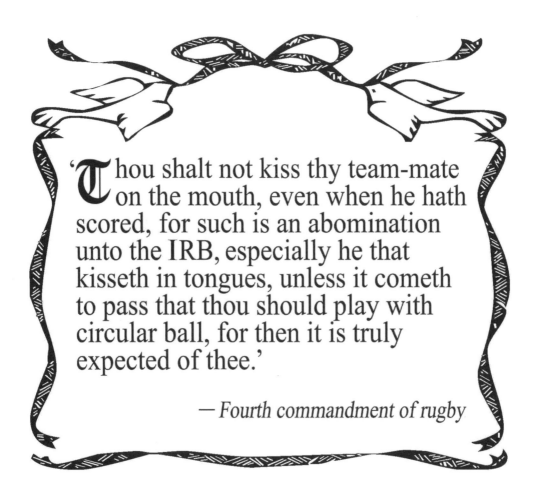

'Thou shalt not kiss thy team-mate on the mouth, even when he hath scored, for such is an abomination unto the IRB, especially he that kisseth in tongues, unless it cometh to pass that thou should play with circular ball, for then it is truly expected of thee.'

— *Fourth commandment of rugby*

'Thou shalt not pass the ball to a brother thy team-mate about to be smashed by thine enemies, unless it be known to all men that he oweth you money, or hath porked someone dear to your heart, in which case all shall be forgiven and then, verily, thou mayest pass to him right slowly and on high.'

— *Ninth commandment of rugby*

'Geez, this fitness thing has got complicated. I just run my blokes till they spew and then take 'em down the pub.'

— *Butch McDougal*

'What do you get out of it? You get a sore hand and a week's break.'

— *Richie McCaw, on why he doesn't punch opponents*

'Rugby and sex are the only things you can enjoy without being good at them.'

— *Anonymous*

'Rugby players are like lava lamps: good to look at but not very bright.'

— *Anonymous*

'I don't know why props play rugby.'

— *Lionel Weston*

'Forwards are the gnarled and scarred creatures who have a propensity for running into and bleeding over each other.'

— *Peter FitzSimons*

'Whoso would be a man, must be non-conformist and preferably play in the pack.'

— *Ralph Waldo Emerson*

'Ja, anyone know where I can get an engine for a Toyota Corolla?'

— *Frans Erasmus, late Springbok prop, on being asked if he had anything to add to an inspiring team talk*

HOW THE FORWARDS SEE THE BACKS

The forwards: eight handsome, burly guys whom you'll gladly give your beer and food to, and you'd want to marry your daughter. They are intelligent, elegant, sensitive and sweet. Truly the ideal men.

The backs: seven guys who will steal your beer, take advantage of your women folk, barnyard animals and all tubular household objects, regularly take blow dryers on road trips, and wear bikini underpants.

— *Rugby positions*

HOW THE BACKS SEE THE FORWARDS

'Look, these Phantom comic-swappers and Mintie eaters, these blond-haired flyweights are one thing and we will need them after the hard work's done. But the real stuff's got to be done right here by you blokes.'

— Ross Turnbull, addressing the Wallabies' forwards on the merits of their backs

'Forwards win games, backs decide by how much.'

— Planet Rugby

'Colin Meads is the kind of player you expect to see emerging from a ruck with the remains of a jockstrap between his teeth.'

— *Tony O'Reilly*

'She reckoned pasta was the best thing to have. Ha! If that were true, the Italians would be world champs but they're bloody useless.'

— *Sir Colin Meads*

(Commenting on the All Blacks' dietitian's advice for a pre-match meal)

'Everybody thinks we should have moustaches and hairy arses, but in fact you could put us all on the cover of *Vogue*.'

— *Helen Kirk, US rugby player*

'Whoever said giving birth is the worst pain there is has never seen her team lose the World Cup.'

— *Bumper sticker*

'The number of people who say, "Why don't you smile when the camera is on you?" At least you're not scratching your balls.'

— *All Blacks coach Graham Henry*

'You guys pair up in groups of three, then line up in a circle.'

— *Colin Cooper, Hurricanes coach*

'Lions tours used to represent the apogee in the kind of behaviour usually regarded as hooliganism if perpetrated by the lower orders but high-jinks if it involves young gentlemen of quality.'

— *Matthew Engel, the* Financial Times

'How did the referee determine when a foul had been committed given that all the players were beating the crap out of each other more or less continuously?'

— *Toby Young, the* Spectator

'You've got to get your first tackle in early, even if it's late.'

— *Ray Gravell*

'Right, lads, I want 80 per cent commitment for 100 minutes.'

— *Noel Murphy*

'Most footballers are temperamental. That's ninety per cent temper and ten per cent mental.'

— *Doug Plank*

Murray Deaker: 'Have you ever thought of writing your autobiography?'

Tana Umaga: 'On what?'

'Fa'– nickname of Scott Quinnell.

'Everyone knows that I've been pumping Martin Leslie for a couple of seasons now.'

— *Murray Mexted*

'Nobody in rugby should be called a genius. A genius is someone like Norman Einstein.'

— *Jono Gibbes*

'What is it with you? Is it ignorance or apathy? He said, "I don't know and I don't care." '

— *David Nucifora talking about Troy Flavell*

'I want to reach for 150 or 200 points this season, whichever comes first.'

— *David Holwell*

'The relationship between the Welsh and the English is based on trust and understanding. They don't trust us and we don't understand them.'

— *Dudley Wood*

'Mothers keep their photo on the mantelpiece to stop the kids going too near the fire.'

— *Jim Neilly, on the Munster pack*

'Look what those bastards have done to Wales. They've taken our coal, our water, our steel. We've been exploited, raped, controlled and punished by the English ... and that's who you're playing this afternoon.'

— Phil Bennett

'I knew he'd never play for Wales ... he's tone deaf.'

— Vemon Davies, explaining his son's choice to play for Wales

It may be time to hang up the boots when ...

Your six-pack has turned into a keg.

You look at taking out a restraining order against your opposite number.

You get winded watching the game plan.

'Rugby players are either piano shifters or piano movers. Fortunately, I am one of those who can play a tune.'

— *Pierre Danos, French player*

'You pay the piano player as much as you want but if you don't pay the piano pusher then the concert doesn't happen.'

— *Dan Crowley, former Australian prop, on player payments*

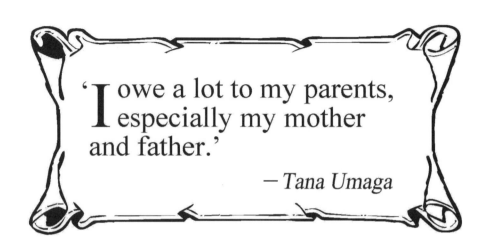

'I owe a lot to my parents, especially my mother and father.'

— Tana Umaga

'I had all the brand new gear right down to the boots with clean white laces. When we got there the coach decided I was too young to play. My mum took me home in tears. I was so upset she let me sleep in my gear that night.'

— Todd Blackadder, aged six

68

'He's not the sharpest knife in the draw, our Jeremy. He still gets confused why his sister has two brothers but he's only got one.'

— Andy Nicol on Jeremy Guscott

'A splendid type and a good rugby player... he is virtually bone from the neck up and needs things explained in words of one letter.'

— British Dominion Office, 1964, describing East African forward Idi Amin

'I think he's broken his nose.'

— *First commentator, as Sean Fitzpatrick is being led from the field*

'No, I think someone has broken it for him.'

— *Second commentator
(Fergus Slattery)*

'Will there be many of them?'

— *Willie John McBride, on being told by an Afrikaans publican that he was calling the police*

72

'No leadership, no ideas. Not even enough imagination to thump someone in the line-out when the ref wasn't looking.'

— *J.P.R. Williams on a Welsh loss*

'How's Stirling Mortlock's nuts?'

— *Female reporter questions Eddie Jones on Mortlock's groin injury*

'The winners eat the losers.'

— *A Fijian player answers an English reporter's question, 'How do you celebrate a victory?'*

'My father used to call that not a tactical kicker but a testicle kicker…basically a real balls-up.'

— Murray Mexted

'Don't hit him in the honeymoons.'

— Andre Watson, referee

'F*** you!'
— Player to French referee Didier Mene

'What did you say?' *— Mene*

'I said "F*** you!"' *— Player*

'I'll decide who f***s me. You're off!'
— Mene

'Rugby football: Each side is allowed to put in a certain amount of assault and battery and do things to its fellow man which, if done elsewhere, would result in 14 days without the option, coupled with some strong remarks from the Bench.'

— *P.G. Wodehouse*, Very Good, Jeeves, *1930*

'A bomb under the West car park at Twickenham on an international day would end fascism in England for a generation.'

— *Philip Toynbee, British writer and communist*

'Brian, what are you going to do for a face when Saddam wants his arse back?'

— *Peter Clohessy to opposing prop Brian Moore*

'The first half will be even. The second half will be even harder.'

— *Terry Holmes*

'This is a rugby ball, right?'

— *Ciaran Fitzgerald, Irish captain, attempts to simplify a dressing-room talk*

'Oh Jesus! You're going too fast for us.'

— *Voice from the back*

'The Holy Writ of Gloucester Rugby Club demands: first, that the forwards shall win the ball; second, that the forwards shall keep the ball; and third, the backs shall buy the beer.'

— *Doug Ibbotson*

'The pub is as much a part of rugby as is the playing field.'

— *John Dickenson*

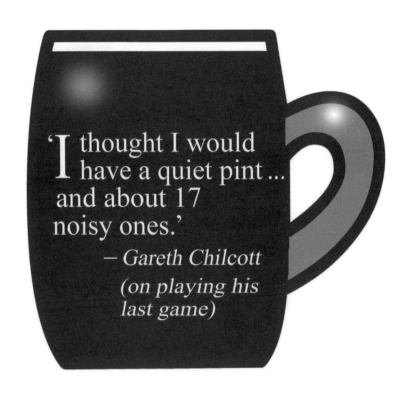

'I thought I would have a quiet pint ... and about 17 noisy ones.'
— *Gareth Chilcott* *(on playing his last game)*

'Beer was invented to stop props taking over the world.'

— *Anonymous*

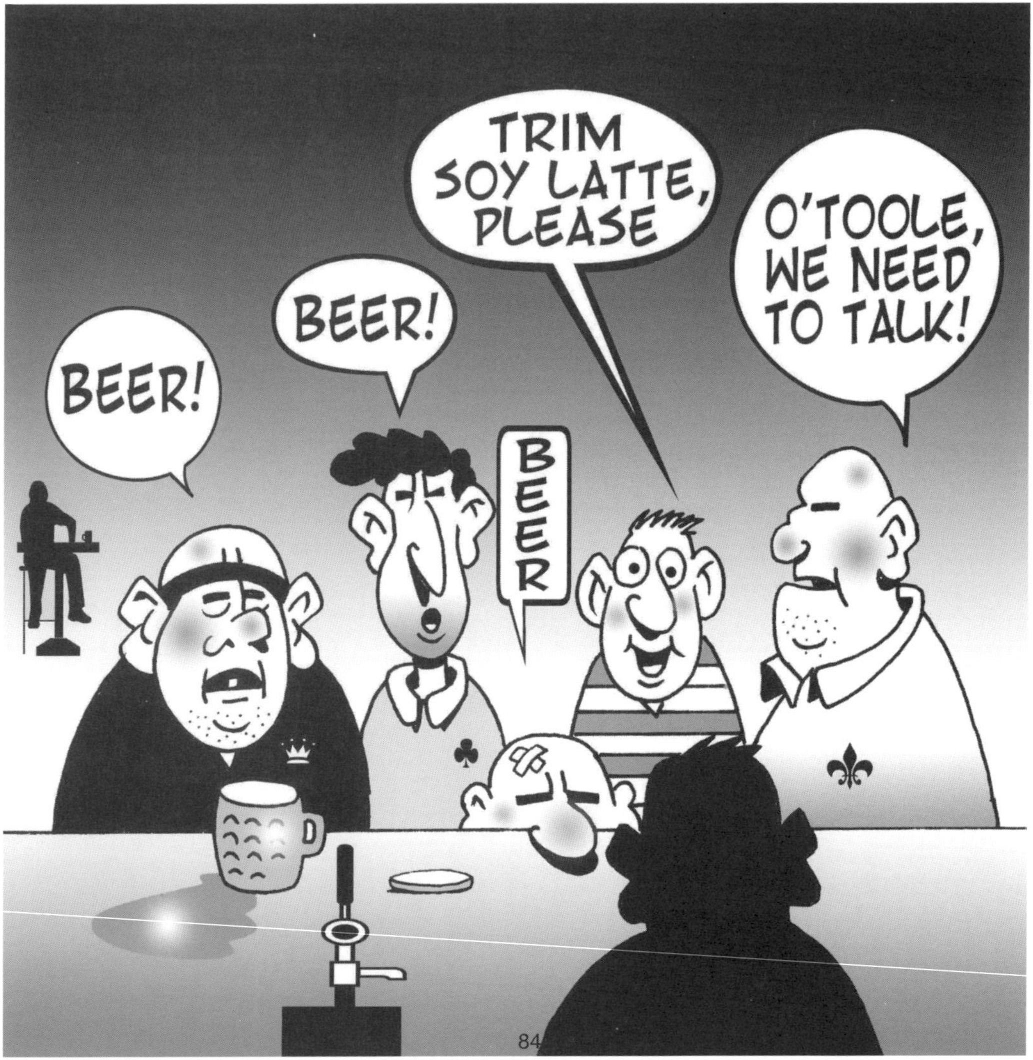
BEER!
BEER!
BEER
TRIM SOY LATTE, PLEASE
O'TOOLE, WE NEED TO TALK!

'To play rugby league you need three things: a good pass, a good tackle and a good excuse.'

— Anonymous

'The main difference between playing league and union is that now I get my hangovers on Monday instead of Sunday.'

— Tom David

'Rugby league is a simple game played by simple people. Rugby union is a complex game played by wankers.'

— Laurie Daley, former league player

'**B**acon and eggs: the chicken is involved, the pig is committed!'

> *— Alan Jones, former Wallaby coach, giving the team some food for thought*

'**W**e had a personality clash. He didn't have one.'

> *— Peter FitzSimons on Alan Jones*

'**C**'mon, Stan! Movement is good for weight loss!'

> *— Alan Jones to Stan Pilecki*

'**Y**ep, and you're living proof. No double chin!'

> *— Pilecki's reply*

'We are not calling them the All Blacks this week. They are New Zealand. New Zealand is a poxy little island in the South Pacific.'

— Scott Johnson, then Welsh assistant coach

'I apologise to all New Zealanders. In fact, it's *two* poxy islands in the South Pacific.'

— Johnson again

'The job of the Welsh coach is like a minor part in a Quentin Tarantino film: you stagger on, you hallucinate, nobody understands a word you say, you throw up, you get shot.'

— *Mark Reason*

'Nobody ever beats Wales at rugby. They just score more points.'

— *Graham Mourie*

'There's nothing that a tight forward likes more than a loosie right up his backside.'

— *Murray Mexted*

'He deserved it.'
— Brad Johnstone,
Italian coach, on why
Peter Stringer was
headbutted by his prop

'Rugby is a mimic war. When we want real war, we turn to the front of the newspaper.'

— *Simon Barnes,* The Times

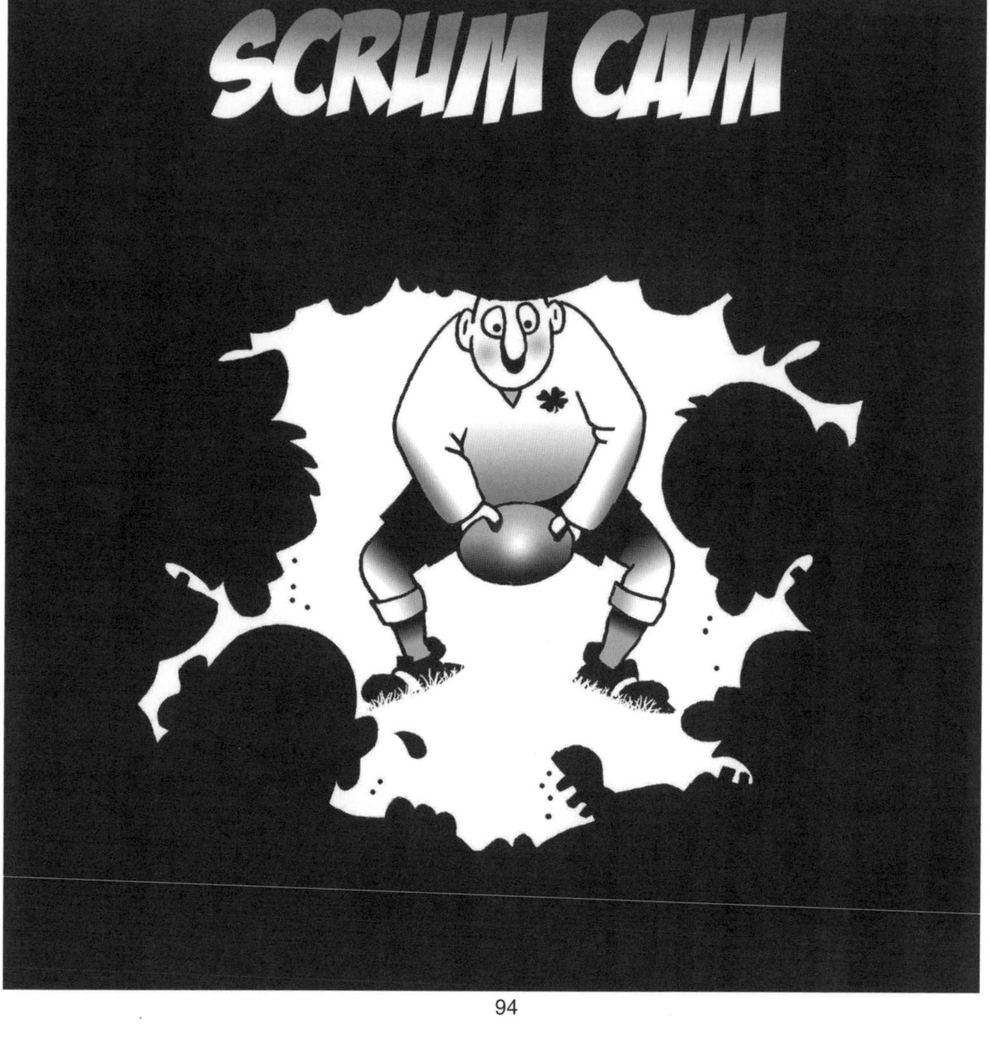
SCRUM CAM

'The front row is an immensely technical place where brain and brawn collide; it is one which has fascinated me since I played a prop whose shorts caught fire during a game as a consequence of carrying a light for his half-time fag.'

— *Bill Lothian,* Edinburgh Evening News

'Rugby people. Can't live with them. Can't shoot them.'

— *Tom Humphries,* The Times

'Could have been any one of 29 of us.'

— Harlequins player, when quizzed by the referee as to who punched Will Carling

'You have 15 players in a team. Seven hate your guts and the other eight are making up their mind.'

— Jack Rowell

'It's no good to talk like Tarzan and play like Jane.'

— Keith Andrews

> '**W**hat's that thing on his head?'
>
> — *Garrick Morgan asks a team-mate while watching Mikhail Gorbachev on TV*
>
> '**I**t's a birthmark.' — *Fellow player*
>
> '**H**ow long's he had that?'
>
> — *Morgan*

'**E**very time a player like Garrick Morgan leaves rugby to go to rugby league, it lifts the IQ of both codes.'

— *Martin Johnson*

100

'Cliff, this must have been a very disappointing result for the All Blacks.'

'Well, they've had very bad luck on tour so far. They missed four easy kicks against the Exeter Amateur Operatic Society, and then of course there was that crippling defeat at the hands of the Derry & Toms soft toy department, so I don't think they can really be fancying their chances against the London Pooves on Saturday.'

— Monty Python's Flying Circus, *Episode 23.*
Interviewer: Michael Palin; Cliff: Graham Chapman

'A game played by fewer than 15 a side, at least half of whom should be totally unfit.'

— *Michael Green*

'Right! Which ones are the All Blacks?'

— *Overheard in a corporate box at Twickenham before an England – New Zealand game*

'Wife or World Cup? I'm going to miss her.'

— *South African supporter's banner outside Stade de France, 2007*

'I once dated a famous Australian rugby player who treated me just like a football: he made a pass, played footsie, then dropped me as soon as he scored.'

— *Kathy Lette*

'In America a guy might wake his partner in the middle of the night to make love. A Kiwi would wake her up to watch the All Blacks on TV.'

— *Female reporter, London's* Daily Telegraph

'That is blatantly wrong! Any sensible Kiwi would wake his partner and get her to organise the tea and biscuits so she could watch the game with him.'

— *Keith Quinn*

'Rugby is a good occasion for keeping thirty bullies far from the centre of the city.'

— *Oscar Wilde*

'Those who can play games, they play. Those who can't play, coach. Those who can't coach, write. And those who can't write, commentate!'

— *Jim Neilly, BBC commentator*

'Bill, there's a guy just run on the park with your backside on his chest.'

— Steve Smith to Bill Beaumont, as Erica Roe streaked at Twickenham

---

'He'd certainly be in the starting line-up for the Easter Island first 15.'

— Phil Kearns commenting on the size of Schalk Burger's head

'Paddy, do you realise you're depriving a village back home of an idiot?'

— Eric Rush, to referee Paddy O'Brien

'Do that again, son, and you will live up to your name.'

— *Gareth Chilcott to Dai Young*

'Rugby is played by men with odd-shaped balls.'

— *Bumper sticker*

'He scored that try after 22 seconds – totally against the run of play.'

— *Murray Mexted*

'Get your retaliation in first!'

— *Willie John McBride*

'American football is rugby
after a visit from a health
and safety inspector.'

— *Anonymous*

'Beating NSW is like sex: when it's
good, it's great and when it's not,
you can always get on the piss.'

— *Chris Handy*

'Rugby backs can be identified because they generally have clean jerseys and identifiable partings in their hair... come the revolution, the backs will be the first to be lined up against the wall and shot for living parasitically off the work of others.'

— *Peter FitzSimons*

'He trudg'd along unknowing
what he sought,
and whistled as he went,
for want of thought.'

> — The Referee,
> *by John Dryden*

'Grandmother or tails, sir?'

> — *Referee to Princess Anne's
> son, Peter Phillips, on the
> pre-match coin toss*

'I can't remember the names
of all the clubs that we went to.'

*— Chris Masoe of the Hurricanes on
whether he'd visited the pyramids
on his visit to Egypt*

'Now spread out, lads, and stick
together.'

— Noel Murphy, former Ireland captain

'I've never had major knee surgery
on any other part of my body.'

— Jerry Collins

'To win, their 15 players have to have diarrhoea and we will have to put snipers around the field shooting at them and then we have to play the best game of our lives.'

— *Argentine lock, Juan Martin Fernández Lobbe, on playing the All Blacks*

'Like 15 mongrel dogs outside a butcher shop.'

— *Chris 'Buddha' Handy describes the All Blacks*

'They say you learn a lot more out of losing than winning. Well, they've learnt a lot this year.'

— *Greg Martin, on the Brumbies 2011 season*

'It was not possible for my players to turn the other cheek, as that was being punched as well.'

— *Eddie 'Bones' Jones, Welsh manager of Pontypridd, on a post-match pub brawl with French club Brive*

'And there we see the sad sight of Martin Offiah limping off with a broken finger.'

— *Ray French*

UM, I THINK YOU MAY HAVE SOMETHING THAT BELONGS TO ME

I WONDER IF THEY PLAY RUGBY ON GOOGLE EARTH

BLOODY NIGHT GAMES!

'Far be it for me to criticise the referee, but I saw him after the match and he was heading straight for the opticians. Guess who he bumped into on the way? Everyone!'

— *Ian McLauchlan*

'Soccer is about spending 90 minutes pretending that you're injured. Rugby is about spending 80 minutes pretending that you're not.'

— *Anonymous*

126

'I know why they call rugby the game they play in heaven. Because it bores you to death.'

— *James Hooper, the* Sunday Telegraph

'Spencer's running across the field calling out, "Come inside me, come inside me." '

— *Murray Mexted*

'**R**ugby is nonsense, but a serious nonsense.'

— *Cliff Morgan*